POEMS BY MARY ROGERS-GRANTHAM

Under a Daylight Moon

Copyright © 2013 by Mary Rogers-Grantham
Cover Sky Artwork by Genevieve "Gigi" Girouard
Cover Design by Janelle Smith
Cover template by Alexandra King

All rights reserved.
Printed in the United States of America
For permission to reproduce selections from this book, write to:

Merlee
1287 West Gregory Boulevard
Kansas City, MO 64114
ISBN-13: 978-0-9793362-2-5

Published by:

MRK Publishing
PO Box 353431
Palm Coast, FL 32135

Also by Mary Rogers-Grantham

It's Okay: Poetic Memoirs
Clear Velvet
Rotating Reflections: A Poetry Trio

I have come to believe over and over again that what is most important to me must be spoken, made verbal and shared, even at the risk of having it bruised or misunderstood. — Audre Lorde

Contents

Conversation with a Poem 1
Come On, Now 2
Survivor 3
December River 4
Under a Daylight Moon 5
River Cabin 6
Johnson Grass 7
Barefoot Innocence 8
The Four O'Clocks Whisper 9
Good Night, Iris 10
Saturday Anthem 11
Mother 12
In Reverse 13
Noah's Coffee House on the River 14
Puréed Whiskey Shots at Dawn 15
Martyr Anonymous 17
Naked Blues 18
Green Tea Popsicles 19
Fantasies in E Flat Major 20
Sun Tea for Mosquito Bites 21
Glistening Necklace 22
Girl Child 23
First Friday Stilettos 24
An Hour with Regalia 25
Moon Remnants 26
The Dead Pecker Bench 27
Drafting 28
I'm Just-Saying 29
Ten Tall Seasons and Then Some 30
Better Than Well 31
Still Life 32

Acknowledgements

These poems appeared in the following publications in which some were earlier versions:

And/Or
"Green Tea Popsicles"

Touch Poetry
"The Four O'Clocks Whisper"

Number One
"Noah's Coffee House on the River"
"Puréed Whiskey Shots at Dawn"

Present Magazine
"Ten Tall Seasons and Then Some"

Everyday Poems
"Under a Daylight Moon"

Rougarou
"Barefoot Innocence"

The Goldstein Memorial Merit Award

"Drafting"

Under a Daylight Moon

Conversation with a Poem

Speak to me, Poem…I'm searching…for what no one understands…Are you doing time, Poem…a lot of poems do time…like women who inflict wrath on their no good baby daddy…do no good poems desert their lovers…

Do no good poems ever apologize…no good poems get confused…because they are always looking to be found…like wanted posters…*Have You Seen Me* captions …and blues guitars at midnight…looking for a poem to take home…

I know poems get rejected…like disco music in 1970s clubs and the choir opening church service with Dry Bones…people forget their origin…what helps them make it over…what protects them…and what's on the other side of through…

Share your plans, Poem…you can tell me…I hear you're a hip-hop artist…a filmmaker… working hard to earn recognition…like a Grammy…you ever miss home…talk to me, Poem… we'll discover what no one understands.

Come On, Now

Where I come from
poetry grows wild along highways.
Words marinate in shopping malls,
and titles emerge at first light.

Where I come from
blues breed Hallelujahs.
Hosannas nest in the wind,
and prayers are poetry at work.

Where I come from
pantoums narrate events,
headlines become found poems,
and haiku gives birth to nature.

Survivor

—*A Haiku*

Sultry summer night.
A basketball smacks concrete.
He misses his friend.

December River

Late evenings in August
I sit in the backyard swing,
close my eyes, and pretend

I'm wearing a snow-crocheted camisole,
an icicle thong, and frosted sandals.

A drooping mimosa shades me.
Its blooms, like handmaids,
dab the sweat from my chest.

Leftover daylight paints a shimmering spot
on a cornflower blue backdrop.
Totally consumed in a state of musing,
I dive into December River.

Under a Daylight Moon

At noon, a woman plants lilies.
She hums.

The moon is pale,
the sunlight pristine,
an earthworm pushes
through a fresh mound
of black dirt.

The woman stops and inhales spring.
She hums, again.

River Cabin

I lie on his bed and watch the white river

spar with the shore. He lights a candle,

opens a window, and rests beside me

on his bed. Sunset colors our naked bodies.

He outlines mine with his fingertips,

whispers the legend of River Cabin,

and his plan to keep me here. I listen

for the close of the tale that will end

my longing. We are two dandelions

floating on the wind.

Johnson Grass

—After "Eel-Grass" by Edna St. Vincent Millay

Regardless of what I say
    All I really love to feel
Is the sun that brightens the day
    And the Johnson grass in the field
The clay dirt that waits for rain
    In spring and summer seasons
That creates tender grain
    And satisfies nature's reasons.

Barefoot Innocence

I walked barefoot with scorpions,
and played tag with black moccasins—
a twelve-year-old tomboy who climbed trees,

I dipped tadpoles from the bayou,
put them in gallon jars, and then
watched them turn into bullfrogs.

I picked wild berries by the quart,
polished my lips with the red ones, and
stored the rest in the bottom of the fridge.

I dried sweat with berry colored palms,
walked down to the bayou, sat on the bank,
and drowned my fussy feet in cold water.

I felt my first menses warm beneath me
and moved to a cooler spot of bluegrass.
Mosquitoes hummed haloes around my head.

The Four O'Clocks Whisper

Daddy died on the outskirts of sleep
trapped between the smell of evening
and a changeless night.

Mother slept fleshless the rest of her life.

By day,
her dim eyes painted memories on every wall
in the house that Daddy built.
Voiceless prayers filled her nights.
Furious outbursts rested on her lips.
Four centuries of contentment
planted in spring gardens, and flower beds
that only bloomed at four o'clock.
Now, the dust whispers from the earth.

Mother slept fleshless the rest of her life.

Make meaning of endings.
Follow them.

Good Night, Iris

Every day she cared for all in the house
and watched her favorite movie channel at noon.
Every morning she raised all the windows,
opened the screened doors, and shooed
away the lightning bugs.

She laughed at her image in the bottom
of her favorite stainless pot just before
bubbles boiled her silhouette into vapors.
Saturday, she polished tile into sounds of a satin
orchestra, washed toilet bowls into Sunday morning

and waxed hardwood floors that would be
the envy of Hattie McDaniel. And then,
at the end of every day,
her eyes hugged everyone good night,
and her irises tucked them into bed.

Saturday Anthem

—For Grandmama and Grandpapa

Like going to church every Sunday,
I went to their house every Saturday morning.

I inhaled Grandmama's soul
every time she said,
"Morning, Baby."

The living room smelled like Friday night's smothered pheasant
and month old newspapers stacked on the Chippendale chair
that I never sat on.

Instead,
I made my way to my favorite velvet black chair
where I rested my hands on black satin arm covers.

Grandpapa sat in the kitchen across the hall
in his mahogany high chair forcing apple sauce oatmeal
through his cherry grape gums.

Grandmama disappeared deep into the mansion
where she colored her hair blacktop black.
She returned with a huge white comb
protruding through the top of a white cone towel
wrapped around her head.

Mother

I was your baby girl,
remember?
I remember nights in your bed
sleeping so hard that I hoped my breath
would amend my gaffes
and make meaning of Daddy's dreams

while too much grape Kool-Aid peed
on the soft sun dried sheet beneath us.
You washed them in forgiveness
and hung them out to dry in pacific breezes
underneath a navel orange sun.

Sometimes I hear your smile,
smell your soul,
and hug your forgiveness tight.

In Reverse

I choose the booth overlooking the Plaza,
where the sun is piercing the window.
I order a hot pretzel and Oolong tea, and then
watch traffic crawling along the street below.
Groundskeepers pluck the last blooming plants
and bury summer in rich black dirt, but
the rosebushes will remain untouched.

The letters in the store window across the street
are turned backward.

Reminds me of the first time my daughter
met the alphabet. She frowned feverishly
as she pressed and pushed her pencil hard
between the lines on her notebook.
The backward E's and S's made her happy.
Now, I smile as I look at the letters in reverse
and wonder if they make the designer happy.

A shopper standing in front of the window
resembles time staring at itself in the mirror.

Noah's Coffee House on the River

I want to get up one midnight before the moon yawns,
and stars pull the clouds over their heads,
before dew polishes the grass seductive green,
or frost plays heavy metal in the meadow.
I want to hear the first freighter horn
heave through cumulus clouds of fog.
I want to see the first sailboat interrupt dawn
as it rocks past an ancient oil freighter
barely piercing green water.
I want to be the first customer at Noah's Coffee House,
pour my first cup of scalding black coffee,
and find the first line of a new poem in the vapors.

Puréed Whiskey Shots at Dawn

I hurry out to the kitchen
to brew a brutal quart of coffee
to sip while I park and wait.

*I plan to be there to see the first customer
wipe the night from his eyes.*

I pour the scalding energy into my thermos
and drive down to The Place—
the restaurant where Brown Whiskey Shots
lead the list of breakfast beverages on the menu,
followed by
    1 petite order of thick hickory smoked bacon
    2 lightly scrambled organic eggs
    1 slice of buttered Texas Toast
The bold print at the top of the five by nine menu
reads, "Ask the waiter about our hyacinth, caramel,
and chestnut purée whiskey shots."

It's the restaurant where Delbert
hisses orders through his gums,
and Jean Anne, his wife, wears safety goggles
so she can honor orders without routinely
wiping her eyes. Matthew, their son, audits the liquor
and serves it in skinny shot glasses.

I'm pouring a third cup of coffee from my thermos
when the first customer arrives driving an
18-wheeler. She parks her rig on the sandy lot
behind the paved parking lot. Mack International
heaves, burps, and upchucks acid soot from silver pipes.

She reaches to the top of the cab and squeezes a horn
that sounds like an elephant in heat. She swabs her face
with what looks like cotton candy, and then polishes her lips.

She exits Mack and walks into The Place. I follow.
"Hey Jo Rose, your usual is ready," Delbert yells.
He brings her bacon, eggs, and Texas Toast.
Matthew serves her bourbon purée.

6:00
The Place begins to live as customers file in,
wipe the night from their eyes,
and order the Jo Rose Special, and
I wonder if this is Resurrection Day.

Martyr Anonymous

He moves through Friday night
as quiet as thirst
while sassafras makes love
to the row of cypress trees
beneath her fourth floor loft.

One minute past midnight
the Saturday morning martyr
stands beneath a cypress
hurling daunting one liners
and sneezing illicit phrases

into a night blacker than onyx.
Cleanse Me.

Naked Blues

The piercing shrill from an ambulance
whines through the dingy morning light—
sifting her thoughts through shadows
of horror which she wants to forget.
She rolls out of her sleeping bag, sits upright,
and wipes tired from her eyes.

Tears cover her brilliant auburn freckles
as she rolls the bag into a scroll
and fastens it to the harness on her back.
Once she slept in the comfort of home.
The sting in her throat keeps the mad inside,
as she shuffles memories into naked blues.

Green Tea Popsicles

This is the year to obey flashing stop signs,
choose paper at the grocery checkout,
and leave the plastic for dog owners.

This is the year to revisit a favorite classic,
read your favorite poem aloud, and
tattoo the first line on your shoulder.

This is the year to make green tea popsicles,
prepare martini yogurt using nonfat milk,
and drink Skinny Girl Sangria.

Fantasies in E Flat Major

Aged sun shines through crystal vases and Eve draws Jack Daniels from a well. Beethoven sits in a sailboat pantomiming Symphony No. 5, and George Stevens reads "The Greatest Story Ever Told" to dinosaurs in Jurassic Park. Abraham grills a beast in the shade of an olive tree while Sarah suns on Queen Anne's lace. The Red Sea is littered with water maples waltzing to "The Art of Fugue." I close my eyes and tuck my minor fantasies into E flat major.

Sun Tea for Mosquito Bites

Out in the rural countryside,

the landscape is an endless echo to the sun.

Discourse is literally delightful and the air outside is organic.

Amazing yellow vegetables emerge from black dirt,

a byproduct of meadow muffins and compost harvests.
                         Yellow tomatoes, yellow peppers, yellow melons.

Female mosquitoes feed on nectar,

their blood drives never scheduled.

Sun tea swabs take the itch out of the bite.

Glistening Necklace

Dark clouds hang over traffic like wet denim on a clothesline. Shimmering head beams and traffic lights adorn the dawn with a necklace. Travelers heading west turn up the volume on the radio to listen to weather updates, except one traveler driving a ragtop whose head bobs up and down to Beyonce's "To the Left, To the Left." He turns left onto a side street. Lightning waves through the sky and sheets of rain dare anxious drivers. Miniature rivers ripple through the streets and invade gutters, while hail plays Ping-Pong on car hoods. Tree branches break and fall, and helpless daffodils hang their heads to a waterlogged earth that heaves its excess into neighboring yards. Flat bottom cumulus clouds quarrel with the sun, and then the glistening morning subsides.

Girl Child

Flying far above the seasoned oak in the backyard,
two blue jays lament, and the December morning
embrace their echoes. Two mourning doves huddle
on the back porch side-by-side.

A nine-year-old girl child is sold into marriage.
She is divorced by age ten.
I wonder whether her father has any remorse.

If blue jays could talk,
they would give voice to the shame.
If mourning doves could cry,
they would grieve for the girl child.

And Beethoven's Symphony No. 3
would call her, Eroica.

First Friday Stilettos

This morning she's stepping her way to
first Friday lecture and workshop.
She struts down Garland Avenue in stilettos
that dare not respond to her swag.
She moves the skinny heels along the sidewalk
like a sex goddess on a runway.

She struts down Garland Avenue
in stilettos that respond to her swag.
Each shoe touches the sidewalk like
two stepping on an ice field.
Inside the pouch that drips off her shoulder
is a black velvet outfit, a halter stud bra
and a matching hip belt. It's the one
she wears to Le'Moan, the place where
she swivels, twists, and thumps her hips
on first Friday nights—
where attendance is super sized
and last month's blues rise and fall
to the rhythm of her dance.

An Hour with Regalia

Regalia, a regular, sits at the end of the bar
and draws circles in the bottom of a vintage glass
with a ceramic celery stirrer. He's drinking a Bloody
Mary and eating stuffed jalapenos.
He talks to the bartender about
a couple of his favorite classics—
"Fall of the House of Usher" and
"The Most Dangerous Game."
Regalia's storytelling moves to the rhythm
of the bartender's orders— steady.
An hour later, he pays his tab
and warns the bartender next Friday
will be "The Gift of the Magi."

Moon Remnants

> When the yellow warbler sings,
> daylight seems lighter,
> and hours lengthen across the morning.

When furious winds agitate the evergreen
at night, the moon appears to leap
between trees that move with the wind.

> Pigeons perch there during the day,
> and roost there at night.
> This year they'll breed at The Cathedral.

The Dead Pecker Bench

Every Saturday they sit on double benches
along the street that runs through town.
They spit their week through spaces where
teeth once stood in the seedtime of their lives.
They watch tight tails in blue jeans
swinging from side-to-side,
back and forth like the cadence of a two-stepper.
Irregular seams in their faces are buried storylines.
They wipe sweat from their temples and rest a hand
on the portal of their pants, while uneven language
falls off the edge of their seats. They capture curves
of swinging breasts and retrieve them at night
while the missus sleeps.

Drafting

The scent of coffee roams the kitchen searching for breakfast—
This morning I'm tired of my alien life
& my stuttering mind.

Today I'm moving to an ancient city
where I can smell the world again
& abandon the echoes of life's gall.

                The first night, I'll sleep beside The Dead Sea
                    & listen to the sounds of dead.

I'm Just-Saying

We
pay monthly bills online,
pay Uncle Sam on time,
select dating sites for playmates,
Christian Mingle for soul mates.

We
send e-cards to celebrate,
find chat rooms to navigate,
buy from Overstock.com,
work online for income@home.

We
like You Tube and Skype,
lose ourselves in Internet hype,
workout with Wii or a TV trainer,
listen to our iPod, a fun no-brainer.

                          Really,
                   I'm just-saying.

Ten Tall Seasons and Then Some

—for Manute Bol

Many times he was too tall
to walk through the average doorframe.
Most of the time he stood in the gap
to help his native Sudan. His smile
was as pure as ivory. His voice filled
Turalei, saturated Sudan, and reminded
the world of civil war in his homeland.
It was the rhapsody in his heart.
Imagine him lumbering through airports
and peering eyes climbing his frame
just to get a glimpse of the stars in his eyes.
Imagine seven feet of hockey on ice,
a seven-foot jockey riding horseback,
a seven-foot boxer in the ring, in the gym,
and in your face. Imagine him as Mother Teresa,
whose selflessness was endless, or Martin Luther
King, Jr., whose determination was ceaseless.
His NBA career can be seen in the eyes
of Sudanese school children. From Kansas to Sudan,
compassion and dignity traveled with him.
Draw a butterfly in the sky, and set it free.

Better Than Well

Professor hands their papers back.
It's the first one she's done
since her senior English class
ten years ago. She tightens her lips,
inhales slowly, deeply, silently.

She turns to the last page of her paper,

gazes at the grade, and then, she
exhales slowly, carefully, silently.
She has done well. Better than well.
She relaxes her lips and lifts her head skyward.
For five seconds, she smiles.

Still Life

In the sanctuary the last song
    flickers like a candle.
The receding river casts the slow
    drought of summer. An epitaph
of dandelion soften the edges of the foot path,
    and when the dust settles at sundown,
I'll imagine Michael playing
    a vintage Hammond
during benediction every Sunday.

www.ingramcontent.com/pod-product-compliance
Lightning Source LLC
Chambersburg PA
CBHW050608300426
44112CB00013B/2132